HAVE YOU HUGGED A MONSTER TODAY?

by Alan Cohen

Illustrations by Keith Kelly

HAVE YOU HUGGED A MONSTER TODAY?

Copyright © 1982 by Alan Cohen
ISBN 0-910367-329

Illustrations by Keith Kelly
Lettering by Barbara Baum
Photograph by Gene Dillman

Rear cover photograph taken at:
   Nature's Holaday Natural Foods Restaurant
   Main Street, Somerville, New Jersey

Costumes furnished courtesy of:
   The Magic Bottle
   23 West Ferry Street, New Hope, Pennsylvania

ALSO BY ALAN COHEN

BOOKS
The Healing of the Planet Earth
The Dragon Doesn't Live Here Anymore
Rising In Love
The Peace That You Seek
Setting the Seen
Companions of the Heart

CASSETTE TAPES
Miracle Mountain
Peace
    with music by Steven Halpern
Deep Relaxation
    with music by Steven Halpern
I Believe in You
    with songs & music by Stephen Longfellow Fiske

Personal Orders:
For a free catalog of Alan Cohen's books, tapes and workshop schedule, write to:

Alan Cohen Publications and Workshops
P.O. Box 450, Kula, Hawaii 96790

Bookstore Orders:
New Leaf
5425 Tulane Drive S.W.
Atlanta, Georgia
30336-2323
(1-800) 241-3829
toll-free number for stores only

To the angels of Light

"If we could read
the secret history of our enemies,
we should find
in each man's life,
sorrow and suffering
enough to disarm all hostility"

—Longfellow

Sometimes the people around us seem like monsters

BUT...

Have you ever thought about
how tough it must be
to be a monster?

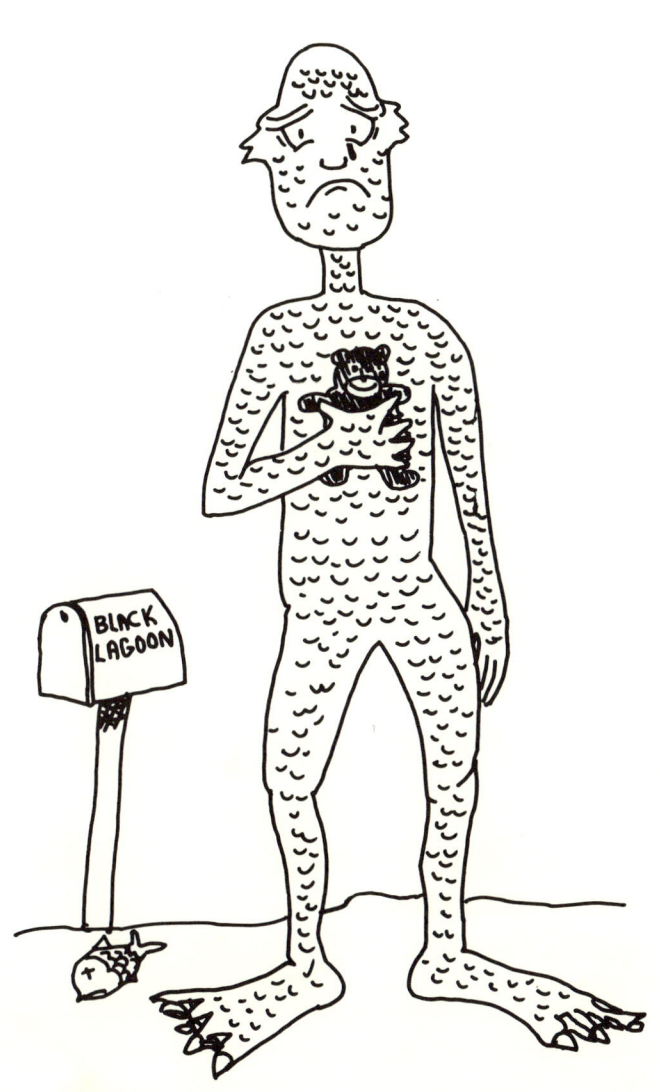

It's not an easy job, you know!

Monsters are really nice people who sometimes lose control of themselves

Gentle creatures who are soft on the inside

That's all monsters are.

Now you don't feel
so afraid of monsters,
do you?

Let's take a look at how monsters got to be the way they are...

(sometimes that helps us to understand them a little better)...

most monsters have had it a little rough in life

They started out as very nice people, but then something happened to them

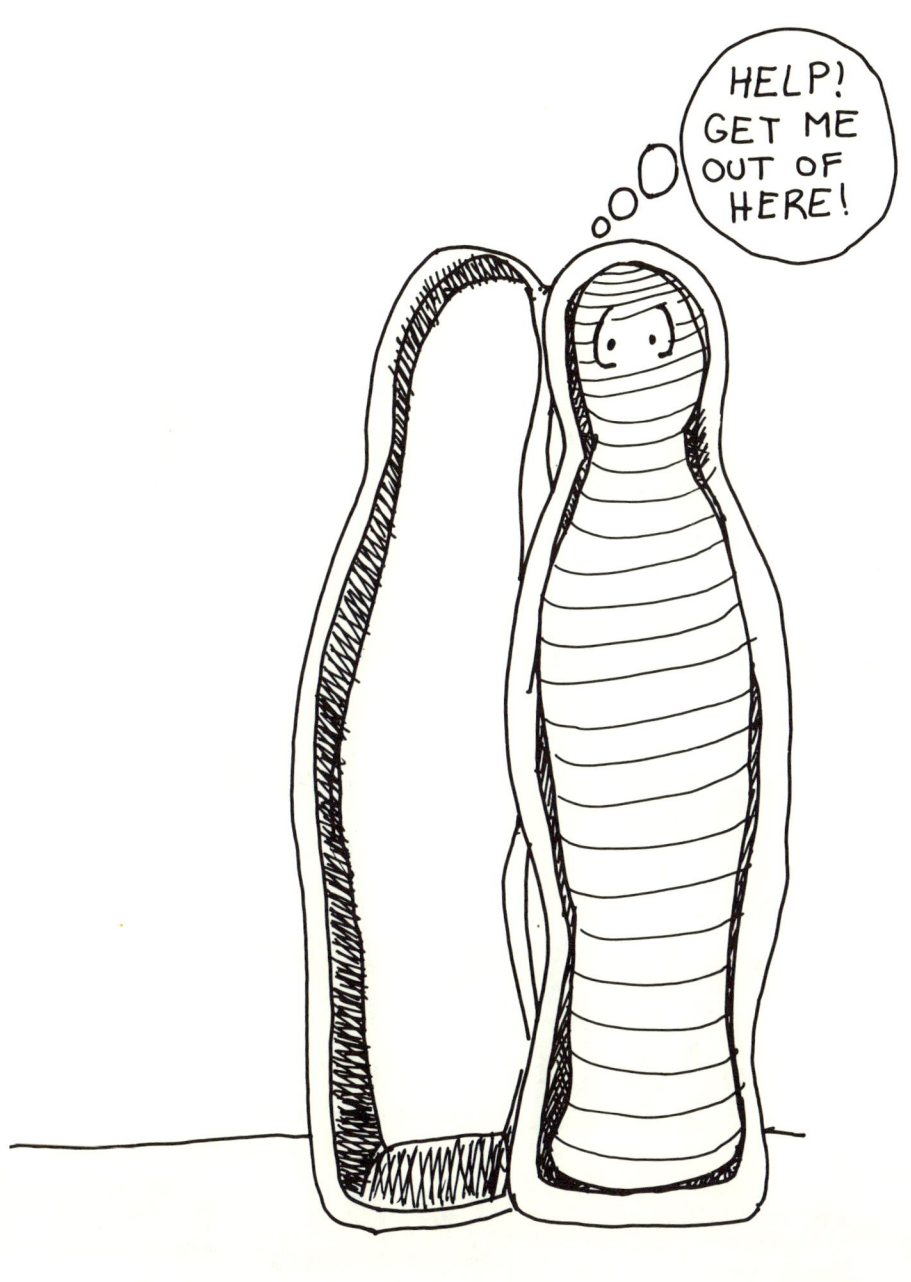

Like we said, being a monster is no easy job!

monsters need love, too!

(... maybe even a little more than you and me)

So the next time
you run into a monster...

when you give a monster
a little love, it will make
him feel so happy that...

it might just remind him of what it felt like to be held in someone's arms

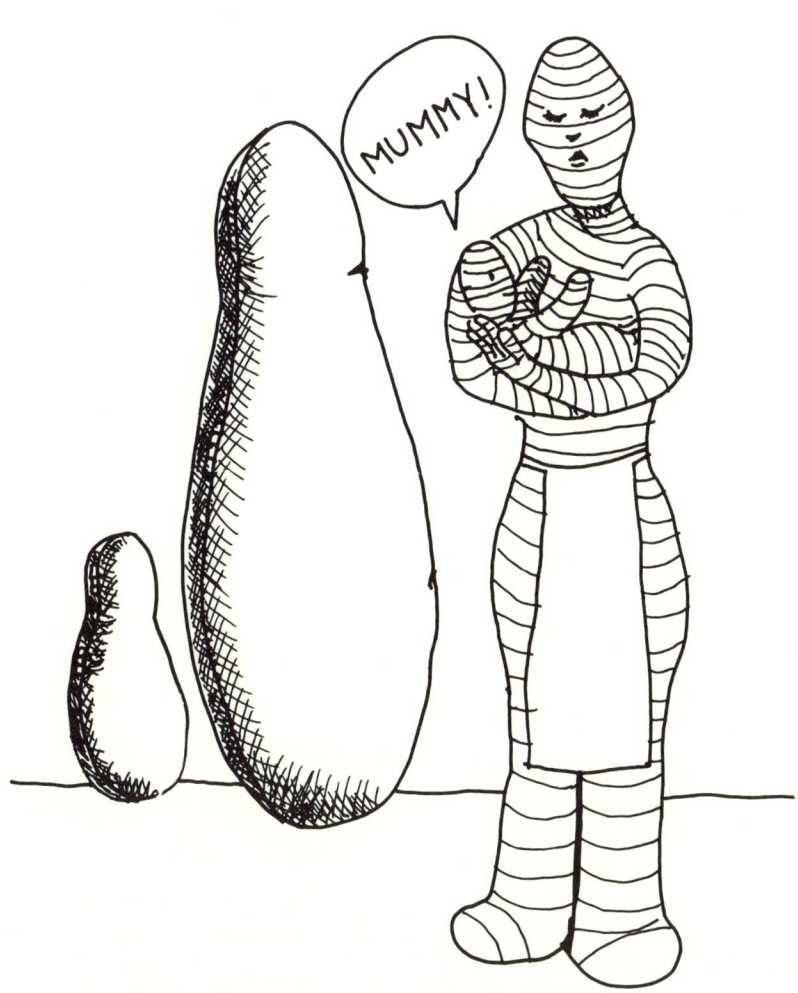

... and, as you know,
that's a very nice feeling

Oh yes —

one more thing

Do <u>YOU</u> ever feel like a monster?

It's not unusual, you know

Not all of us are angels
all the time

Sometimes even the best of people make the silliest mistakes

So the next time
you feel like a monster...

So start with yourself

And then the most amazing thing could happen...

The monsters you hug might just hug the monsters around them

...and they might just hug the monsters around them

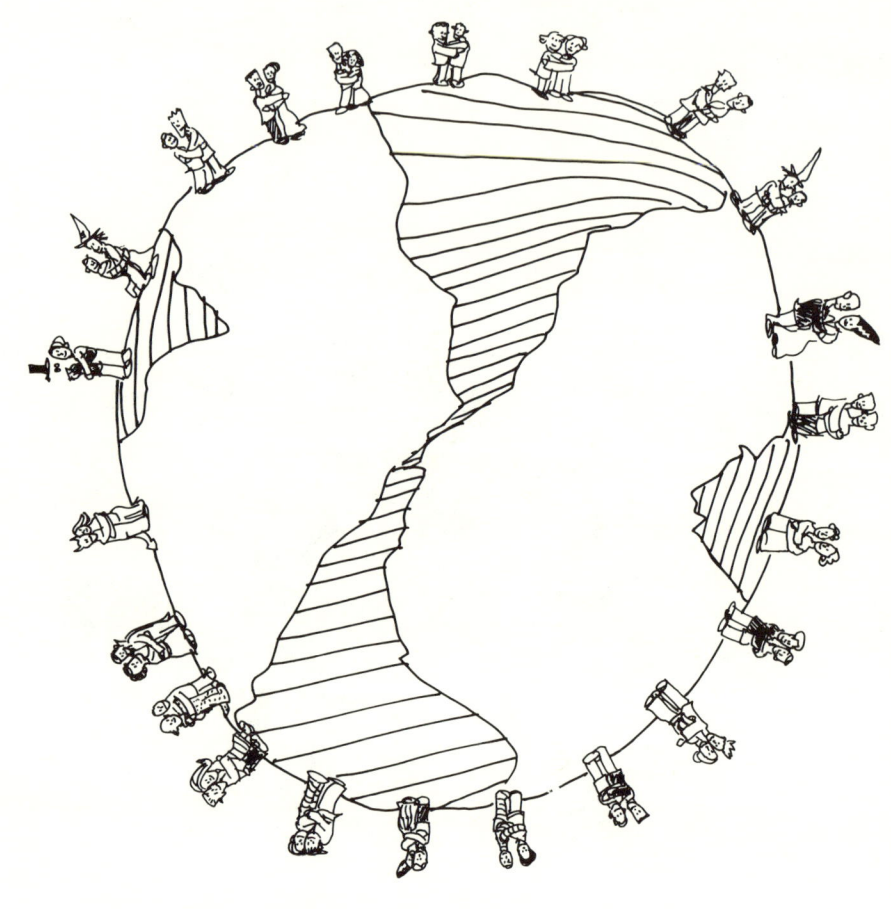

...and hugging monsters might just become the thing that everybody does

And before long,
it may just be that
there will be
no more monsters
because...

and that will be the end of monsters

All because you hugged a monster today

By Alan Cohen
BOOKS

The Healing of the Planet Earth
A golden gift of empowering ideas, an excellent guidebook to give you the courage to release all fear and allow yourself to be lifted naturally to the next stage of personal and planetary transformation. Introduction by Barbara Marx Hubbard, with magnificent photographs by Awakening Heart Productions.

The Dragon Doesn't Live Here Anymore
A bestselling book of encouragement and joyful self-discovery. This warm, open-hearted, and inspiring journey through spiritual growth sheds loving light on self-acceptance, healing, and the power of positive living. A steppingstone and companion to many hearts.

Rising In Love
A touching guide to healing our relationships in the light of love. In a personal, comfortable, and captivating way, Alan offers important, practical insights on how to create fulfilling relationships by believing in ourselves and those we love.

Companions of the Heart
An attractive hard cover volume of the above three popular books. This collection is perfect for those who love to read and re-read these inspiring ideas and to offer as a gift to friends.

The Peace That You Seek
A deeply inspiring and moving collection of channelled messages of guidance, offered as gifts to the Children of Light on the threshold of a New Age. These messages offer great strength, wisdom and caring, shared to serve as healing reminders of the wonder that shines within us. A special gift for the spirit.

Have You Hugged A Monster Today?
A delightful story that teaches how to discover the hearts of the meanest monsters and make friends with the friendless. Shared through clever, laughable cartoons and captions, this is an entertaining course in human relations for children of all ages. Illustrations by Keith Kelly.

Setting the Seen
A series of fascinating guided visualizations for deep relaxation and stress management. Written with instructions for use by teachers, counselors and those in the healing profession, this is a practical guide to physical, emotional and spiritual tranquility. (Companion to cassette *Peace*)

CASSETTE TAPES

Peace
A soothing tapestry of guided images, excellent for meditation, relaxation and personal growth. Useful for spiritual growth, awakening creativity and mental clarity. Alan Cohen's voice blends with Steven Halpern's music to create a deep harmony of being that will touch you in a most important way.

Deep Relaxation
A one-hour program of exercises to relax, renew and reinvigorate. Excellent for those who would like to practice yoga at home; this tape guides the listener through a basic series of yoga postures, guided deep relaxation, breathing exercises and meditation. Gentle background music by Dr. Steven Halpern.

Miracle Mountain
A live recording of one of Alan's workshops, in which he invites the participants to become themselves and celebrate their own strength. These tapes capture the essence of Alan's teachings, including many powerfully inspiring moments. Themes include: keys to healing, loving relationships and believing in ourselves. Tapes include songs and music, guided meditations, group interactions and joyous laughter.

I Believe in You
An orchestral journey of self-affirmation, including inspiring, empowering songs by the popular minstrel, Stephen Longfellow Fiske, and a marvelously uplifting guided meditation by Alan. A very moving and practical gift to encourage healing for yourself or others.

* *

Personal Orders:
For a free catalog of Alan Cohen's books, tapes and workshop schedule, write to:

Alan Cohen Publications and Workshops
P.O. Box 450, Kula, Hawaii 96790

Bookstore Orders:
New Leaf
5425 Tulane Drive S.W.
Atlanta, Georgia 30336-2323

(1-800) 241-3829
toll-free number for stores only